Real Stories of People Who Changed the World

This book was Made by:

Kenzie

Jamie

Ada

Sophia

Juniper

Marcia

Raizo

Antea

Mia

Oak

Brianna

Takeda

Jordan

Adrian

Henry

Nica

Ryan

Alex McConduit

Mr. Chernikoff

Arlo Chapple

Table of Contents

What is Activism?

Activism means trying to fix a problem in your community, country, or world. It means seeing a problem and taking action to change it the best that you can. It could be a big problem, or a small problem. You might be an activist for climate change, anti-racism, education, or many other things. It means speaking up for the rights of people, animals and other things around the world. Activism is important because it helps people to know about what is going on in the world and inspires them to help with those problems too. Here are some issues that we care about and want to inspire change for...

One of the most important things I think people should care about is saving animals. They are important because animals give us life. Insects pollinate, bat's give us their poop for fertilizer. We need to help them. Panda's are losing their homes because we are destroying their habitats. If they help us in certain ways we should help them like giving deer rotten apples and look out for animals crossing the road and more. Make sure to look out for them. Thank you, let's save the animal from being extinct!
-Ada

I like and care about all animals. I like dogs the best of all animals. I have two pet beagles, and if you have an animal you probably love it too. I also love animals because they can guard you and protect you. I would like for humans to protect animals like they protect us. For example I think they should add sensors to cars to alert drivers to help avoid hitting an animal.
-Adrian

There are lots of important causes to believe in, but the most important to me is the extinction of the Arctic wolf. One reason this is important to me is because they are my favorite animal. You should think this is important because Arctic wolves help the environment by using "the circle of life". These wolves are dying like the polar bear. Their habitats are destroyed and they are forced to taigas and mesas, which is not where they usually live. In conclusion these wolves are amazing and help the Earth, and they should be saved.
-Antea

I think we should stop littering everywhere in the world because littering can kill animals. Littering can also kill plants. I think littering is ugly. We should pick up the litter and be more careful with our trash.
-Brianna

One of the most important things I think people should care about is pollution. I think it is important to stop pollution because our planet is being polluted which makes so many things unsafe like water and air, just to name a few. You want clean water, safe food to eat, and healthy air to breathe, right? Pollution is making all those things much harder. But we, and many other living things, need those things to be safe so we can live! If we can stop pollution, that can lead us to having a healthy and safe planet again! All you need to do is sew a little bit of Earth's hole, and that one little stitch will have a lasting impact.
-Nica

Everyone in the world should care about animal habitats. The reason this is important to me is that it is sad that people are killing animals' environments. One reason my cause is important is that damaged environments are causing animals to go into extinction. In particular, we should stop chopping down trees and hunting animals just for fur.
-Henry

Climate change is one of the most important issues today. Climate change is melting the ice caps. This makes waters rise, so people will have to move. The ice caps' water will flood coastal cities, towns and islands. Hurricanes will have more water to flood and more power to destroy. You can slow this by choosing electric cars and using green energy.
-Jamie

Everyone in the world should care about animal testing, like testing makeup on animals. It is important to me because animals suffer everyday. If it's not okay for people, why would it be okay for animals? This cause is important because more animals are being hurt everyday. Bunnies are blind and mice are dying. Another reason this cause is important is because animals are forced to live in cages and suffer, never to be cared for like they should be. People should stop buying products where companies test on animals and start supporting companies that don't test on animals. That's what you can do to reinforce no animal testing.
-Juniper

Everyone in the world should care about getting treated fairly since some people get treated fairly and some do not. It is important because women might not get treated fairly and not just women but people that might not have enough money to afford school or shelter and more. Treating people fairly is also called equity. For people that might not get the same stuff as others do it is wrong. Everyone should get paid and treated fairly. It is unfair for someone to have a great time when someone else has to work twice as hard and still not get respected, recognized or even paid. Everyone should get paid as much as the other people do even if they look different. They are the same so treat people the exact same as you would want them to treat you.
-Kenzie

There are over 200 million dogs with no homes at all. We need to give them homes. I really like dogs because they help lots of people like firefighters and blind people. They all need love and homes. Dogs love most people and they like being with us. When dogs are abandoned, they feel lonely and sometimes have no fresh food or water. They can't have dirty food and water because they can get very sick from it and from being cold. If you see a stray dog with no home, call animal control or a shelter.
-Marcia

Everyone in the world should care about the environment and animals. Trees help us breathe, and they also give us food. We also need to give animals homes like forests, because we're not the only ones on Earth. Saving the environment will help us survive. If we don't save forests and things like that, we can't survive. If we destroy animal habitats, the animals wouldn't have anywhere to live, except with us, and we want to give animals a home where they can survive by themselves. You should tell people you know to stop destroying the environment and to save animals.
-Ryan

I want people to stop putting trash in the oceans. This is important to me because animals can die from the garbage. One reason is that trash can kill things like sea critters when they eat the trash. Another reason is people make too much pollution so it makes the animals sick. I want to clean the world up and I believe we can make better places for animals to live in.
-Takeda

World hunger is not a good thing. The poor have starved and others have too, so the more you donate food the more the cause goes down. The more you donate food that's giving the poor food to helping the cause of starvation go down so I'd like to encourage you to try and donate some food. It could be to a school or to other people in need you can donate it to a church or anybody really. I would really like to encourage you to donate food and help stop world hunger.
-Oak

I want to be an activist for animal rights because we need them to help the environment. We need to protect them. They can't help us if they are not here. For example, deer eat a fruit and take out the seeds and put them on the floor and then the seeds grow into a tree or plant. Another reason to protect them is because some of them are endangered species like polar bears. Polar bears' homes are getting destroyed because people are building in their habitats. They are also dying because there is no food for them to eat. A way we can help protect them is by not polluting the water because animals live in the water, and drink it. As you can see there are many reasons why we should protect animals because they are important to the world.
-Mia

Abby Wambach
By Ada & Kenzie

My partner and I will be telling you about the amazing and fantastic Abby Wambach. You might know her from soccer, but we will be telling you about her activism, too. As a kid, Abby's sister had a championship banner in the gym that she played in. Abby always wanted to be a champion like her sister, Beth. She wanted to get redemption since her name was not on that banner. Abby was **persistent** and eventually won a championship just like her sister. She felt so good when she finally got a banner. This made Abby feel good, but she knew she wanted to do even more.

Abby Wambach was born on June 2nd, 1980 in Pittsford, New York. Abby has played many sports. Abby played basketball in high school, and she even made the varsity team, but Abby's heart was set on soccer. She won three soccer championships in high school. She also had three sisters and three brothers for a total of six siblings. Her high school was called Lady of Mercy High School, and she went to college at the University of Florida Gainesville. She is married to Glennon Doyle and her kids are Chase who is 17, Tish who is 14, and Amma who is 12. In 2015, Abby retired from soccer and focused on being an activist.

Abby also works for an International organization called *Right to Play.* This group uses sports as a way to help children in **disadvantaged** areas of the world. Abby has gone to parts of the continent of Africa to meet some of these children. She has worked hard to raise money for the program, as well as in other areas of activism. She wants to be paid as much as male soccer players do and she knows that she or anyone else fighting for these causes can never give up. Abby did not even think of giving up.

Abby Wambach did amazing things on and off the soccer field. She won two Olympic gold medals and the World Cup three times. In 2012, Abby was awarded the Women's Player of the Year honor. Abby was always an amazing player, but she really stepped up in the most important games. Twenty-two of her goals have come in either the World Cup or Olympic Games, and she has twice found the back of the net in an Olympic gold-medal match. Before she retired she had the most goals in women's professional soccer history: 184 soccer goals.

Although Abby and the United States women's team performed better than the male soccer team in competitions like the Olympics and World Cup, the two groups were not paid equally. They didn't earn nearly as much money and got worse treatment than the men did. This not only happened in soccer but in other sports as well. Abby decided to use her voice and fought in a nice way so that female athletes would get paid as much as the men did! When fighting for **equality**, her hard work has paid off for us all.

Not only is Abby Wambach a great soccer player, she is also a great person. She does so many things to help others. Abby showed **perseverance** and courage when she fought for women to get the same treatment and money as the men. She also made sure that children got to play sports in parts of the world where kids rarely get the opportunity to do so. Abby is thoughtful, kind, nice, strong, helpful, and most importantly one of the greatest activists in the world!

Greta Thunberg
By Antea & Juniper

Have you heard of Greta Thunberg? She's a kid who made a big difference in the world. When Greta was 8 years old, she and her classmates learned about climate change. She started to learn more and more about **climate change**. When she was 15, she started strikes to end **global warming**. In 2019, she was the Time Magazine "Person of the Year". If you keep reading, you will learn more about Greta and her goal to change the world.

Greta Thunberg was born January 3rd, 2003 in Stockholm, Sweden. Her family was made up of her mother Malena (an opera singer), her father Svante (an actor), her sister, Beata, and her two dogs. When she was younger, she learned about climate change. She learned the Earth is getting hot. There are more floods and big storms. More animals are going **extinct** (200 per day, in fact), and she wanted to help.

When Greta was young, she was diagnosed with Asperger's Syndrome, which is a type of autism that makes her brain work a little differently than other kids. It gives her a "laser focus" and it helped her learn all she could about global warming and climate change. Greta calls it her superpower, but some kids found her to be shy and snobby because she was quiet. Greta only speaks when she feels it is necessary. Climate change is so important that she was pushed to her limit and needed to speak to the world about it. The school she went to was called Franska Skolan and that is where she began her road to being an **activist**.

A few of Greta Thunberg's greatest accomplishments are getting the government to listen to her and helping the Earth, even though she had some obstacles. Greta's greatest challenges were **politicians** and **fossil fuels**. They were obstacles because the politicians didn't want to listen to her and fossil fuels **pollute** the **environment**. She overcame her obstacles by starting Fridays for the Future, an organization where Greta leads strikes about climate change. Children and adults have joined protests around the world. This is important because she is getting more people to help save the Earth, and she is helping young people's voices be heard by giving them the opportunity to share their beliefs on climate change. Because of her efforts, she won the Gulbenkian Prize for Humanity, and she donated all of her prize money to charity.

Some of Greta's activism includes: believing people can change their habits and helping the Earth. Some ways people can help change the Earth are: stop pollution, plant trees and plants, recycle, and compost. The result of her work was that governments, the United Nations, and people around the world started to listen and make changes to help our Earth. In Ithaca, NY, where we live, the Green New Deal was started as a result of hard work like Greta's. The Green New Deal is a way to help the city of Ithaca reduce its **carbon footprint**. Similar things have been proposed in other cities, states, and for all of the United States.

These accomplishments are going to help make climate change slowly disappear. More animals will be saved, more forests will be saved and our Earth will be saved. Greta says, "No one is too small to make a difference." That means you, yes, you can make a difference! So get out there and no matter where you are, help the earth in any way you can!!!!

Isatou Ceesay
By Alex McConduit

Have you ever had an idea that you thought would make the world a better place? If so, you have at least one thing in common with Isatou Ceesay. As a young girl Isatou grew up in a beautiful place, but that beautiful place eventually ran into an ugly problem... plastic bags! Although these bags found their way into most cities of the world and the average person was able to ignore it, Isatou could not! Eventually she came up with an answer and created a solution that changed her life and her village forever.

Isatou Ceesay was born on December 30th, 1972 in a small village in The Gambia called Njau. She had two sisters and a brother. Her parents were both farmers and all of the kids helped out on the farm. Isatou's father died when she was only 10 years old. When Isatou grew up, her mother couldn't afford to send her to school and so she had to drop out. Even though Isatou didn't get her education from school, she learned a lot on the farm and even more while exploring her village.

While growing up in Njau, Isatou started to see more and more plastic bags littering her village. As she walked to the market, she saw how the bags created a **habitat** for mosquitos and heard stories of animals dying after eating them. One day Isatou saw a goat from her own farm dying from eating a plastic bag and she knew she had to do something. Together with four friends Isatou started the One Plastic Bag movement that educated and encouraged women in her village to recycle plastic waste into things that they could sell for money. They created small hand bags and purses that people from all over the world purchased from them. Isatou's project became famous and people were inspired by her idea. Later on, Isatou created an NGO called The Gambian Women's Initiative that taught women in The Gambia how to recycle peanut shells into fuel. Over 20,000 people work with Isatou's **NGO** and it has helped make The Gambia a more beautiful place. For her hard work Isatou is known as *The Queen of Recycling* all around the world!

Isatou Ceesay was a smart and **courageous** woman. She helped the people around her, even though many of them laughed at her and teased her for "playing with trash". Isatou could have been like other people in her village and ignored the problems the plastic bags were creating, but she didn't. Her ideas and actions not only made her home a better place but also inspired people around the world to follow in her footsteps. If we can all be just a little bit more like Isatou, we will save our planet and make it a better home for the people, plants and animals who live here.

Jane Goodall
By Ryan and Jamie

"Jane, where are you?" exclaimed her mother. Jane was in the hen house for hours watching a chicken! Then Jane ran out and shouted, "I know how an egg comes out." Ever since Jane Goodall was a little girl, she was curious about animals. She had a dream of going to Africa to see wild animals. When she was older, she took a boat to Africa and started her dream. In this book, you will learn all about how Jane Goodall protected the **environment** and helped chimpanzees.

Jane was born on April 3rd, 1934 in London, England and grew up in Waterloo, and she loved animals from a young age. She was **inspired** by Dr. Doolittle, the magician who could talk to animals, and Jungle Book, the story with Mowgli lost in the jungle. She was also inspired by Tarzan, which made her want to be like the Jane in the story. Tarzan's friend, Jane, lived in the jungle, so she wanted to be like her in the jungle. She had a dog named Rusty that she played with all the time. She went to Cambridge University when she saved up enough money and she was older, because she couldn't afford any schools when she was younger. She became an **activist** when she was 43 years old. She had a son named Hugo Eric Louis van Lawick. Hugo's nickname was Grub. She first went to Africa to visit a friend. Next, she found a job there. The job was to research chimpanzees.

Jane wanted to save chimps because they are a lot like humans and people were destroying their habitat. She discovered that chimps use tools and shared behaviors: "So in their communication gestures, kissing, embracing, holding hands, patting one another, begging for food, swaggering, shaking, just using tools, making tools, throwing rocks, in all these ways they behave basically the same as us," explained Jane, "We are not the only beings with personalities… and emotions like joy and sorrow." She got a lot of people to help her save the forests, that not only chimps live in, but other animals, too. She made two programs: *Roots & Chutes* and *the Jane Goodall Institute*. In *Roots & Chutes*, she works with kids to plant trees and other plants. In *the Jane Goodall Institute*, she travels to places all over the world and convinces people to help save the environment and animals.

As you can see, Jane Goodall followed her dream and helped save the world. She was a big help in saving animal habitats. You can be like Jane Goodall and help save the environment and plant trees. You can learn more about Jane in these places: Youtube, The Watcher book by Jeanette Winter, and the CBC Kids News program called "Jane Goodall" on spending her life with chimpanzees. To help with Jane's work, you can plant trees and plants and spread the word about taking care of our environment!

LeBron James
By Adrian, Henry & Raizo

Did you ever want to learn about LeBron James? This book will tell you about LeBron, his life, how he became an activist, and why. We think that he is an awesome person, because he switched teams multiple times and still was great. LeBron also built a school for children who didn't have access to a good education and had few resources to help them get by. These are only a few things LeBron accomplished. He once said, "You have to be able to accept failure to get better." Continue reading to learn more.

LeBron James was born on December 30th, 1984 in Akron, Ohio. He attended school at Vincent-St. Mary High School. James was poor as a child, and his family struggled with money. Eventually, he joined the high school basketball team and worked to become an amazing basketball player. He is such a good basketball player and the NBA wanted him, so they let him skip college to go straight to the NBA. LeBron was only 18 years old. He eventually married his high school sweetheart, Savannah Brinson and they now have three children together named Bronny, Zhuri, and Bryce.

Once LeBron made it into the NBA, he dominated. He won four NBA championships, and he also won a bronze medal in 2004 and a gold medal in both the 2008 and 2012 Olympics. He's won three championships with three different teams; the Miami Heat, the Cleveland Cavaliers, and the LA Lakers. Not only is LeBron an amazing professional basketball player, but he's also done great things for children in need.

LeBron James wrote a book called "I Promise" and made a school with the same name. The school is for kids who may be in **poverty** and don't have a chance to get a good education. The reason he did it was because he wanted to give opportunities to kids without many. He was thirty-five years old when he became an activist. He has used his fame and resources to bring attention to many social issues going on in America and the rest of the world such as the **Black Lives Matter** movement. Even though sometimes it made him unpopular, LeBron continued to try to make things better when he could.

Some people think that being the best basketball player in the world is a big enough accomplishment on its own. Do you? Well, LeBron James does not. He is an activist and even made a school give back to his hometown. Many athletes just focus on themselves and their sport, but LeBron also cares about other people. He made it his mission to make sure children had good opportunities and a great chance to go to college. LeBron James once said, "I think the reason why I am who I am today is because of those tough times when I was younger." LeBron James is a great example that you can **persevere** through hard things and inspire others to never give up.

Malala Yousafzai
By Jordan & Oak

Do you want to change the world? If you do, here are some words that you should live by: "One pen, one teacher and one book can change the world." These are Malala's words. They are some words that we like to live by and some that you should, too. You could even be changing the world right now without even knowing it. Malala Yousafzai is someone who changed the world and if you keep reading you will learn more about how and why.

Malala Yousafzai was born on July 7th, 1997. She was born in Mingora, Pakistan. Her father was a teacher, and she attended the school that he taught at and built. When Malala was eight years old, there was a terrible earthquake, and many of the villages around her were destroyed. Leaders from the Taliban took advantage of the villagers being sad and having their lives in bad shape. They started to try to take over the mountain villages. The villagers were in worse shape as the Taliban grew stronger. The Taliban believed that women and girls should not be allowed to go to school. They did not like that girls like Malala continued to try to get an education.

Originally, Malala wanted to be a doctor, but her dad talked her out of it. He convinced Malala to become an activist instead. Malala made a choice to fight for the right for girls to be educated. Malala spoke out against soldiers from the Taliban who were stopping girls from going to school. At the age of 11, Malala was shot by Taliban soldiers on a school bus. They wanted to stop and silence people like Malala who wanted equal rights. Malala not only survived the attack, she came back even stronger! She was determined for the world to know about the Taliban and the assassination attempts, and she wanted to help every girl in the world get an education.

In 2014, the **Nobel Peace Prize** was awarded jointly to Kailash Satyarthi and Malala Yousafzai for their struggle against the **suppression** of children and young people and for the right of all children to an education. Malala was the youngest person to ever be awarded the Nobel Peace Prize. It was an extra special honor because many young girls in her home never had **access** to an education. Malala used the prize money to start the Malala Fund and began to raise money for girls' education. Malala also used the money to rebuild schools that were destroyed by soldiers.

Malala Yousafzai was a peaceful and heroic young woman. As Malala said in her speech at the United Nations, "We must not forget!". Malala **inspired** the world to always remember to think about others and not just focus on yourself. Malala once said, "When the whole world is silent, even one voice becomes powerful." This makes us feel like we can make a change in the world too.

Naomi Osaka
Brianna, Marcia & Takeda

Do you think you could hit a tennis ball at 125 m.p.h. *and* be brave enough to speak out against **racism**? Naomi Osaka can! She is a professional tennis player who was born in Japan and raised in the United States. She has one of the best serves in tennis. Her serve speed can get up to 125mph. She was ranked number one in the US Women's Open for tennis in 2019. Naomi Osaka is a brave young woman on the court, as well as off the court. She knows how to speak up for what is right.

Naomi was born in Osaka, Japan on October 16, 1997. Naomi's mother is Japanese and her father is Haitian. She started playing tennis when she was very young. Her first goal was to get good enough to beat her older sister, and eventually she did! When she became a little older, Naomi moved to Florida where she attended school at the Broward Virtual School. She competes for the country of Japan and says she identifies with all three nationalities; Japanese, Haitian, and American. Naomi became an activist at the age of twenty, but she always believed in speaking up for what is right.

Naomi Osaka believes in **Black Lives Matter** and that it is important to speak out about it. "You just gotta keep going and fighting for everything, and one day you'll get to where you want", Naomi said. She came up with her own way to speak out against racism. She did this by putting seven names of seven unarmed Black victims who were killed by law enforcement, for seven tennis matches on her face masks which were also Black. When she was asked what message she wanted to send by doing this she said, "I feel like the point was to get people to start talking." She was trying to get people to notice racism and that it is wrong. She wanted people to know that it's not okay to treat someone differently because of their race. Instead of just paying attention to Naomi's tennis skills, the world had to stop and think about the people who had been treated unfairly. Even more amazing than her activism was the fact that she also won the tournaments. Naomi won the US Open and the Australian Open Tennis Competitions. She even won against her hero, Serena Williams, during the US Open in 2020.

In the summer of 2020, Naomi Osaka was on her way to possibly winning another tournament when she refused to play in the next match. She had worked her whole life to become a winner in tennis. Refusing to play was a big risk, but she wanted to bring attention to Black Lives Matter. Naomi Osaka is a very athletic person, but she is brave as well. She has used her fame to help Black Lives Matter and to **inspire** people to talk and think about racism. She continues to study racism and speaks out about it to create more **equity** for all people. Naomi's hard work has made a difference in the world. Naomi once said, "How I came this far is a miracle, but you can, too," and if you work hard to make a difference, you can one day be just like Naomi.

Ruby Bridges
By Mia, Nica & Sophia

Have you ever thought about going to school with only people who look just like you, and don't have many differences than you? Well, you will now when we teach you about the amazing **Civil Rights** activist Ruby Bridges, how much she affected the world, and the difference she made. **Segregation** was a horrible thing, and Ruby Bridges significantly changed that. Continue to read and learn more about what Ruby Bridges did. She became an **activist** at such a young age that she may have not even noticed it.

Ruby Bridges' full name is actually Ruby Nell Bridges. Not a lot of people know her middle name, Nell. She was born in Tylertown, Mississippi on September 8, 1954. She had a big family, and was one of EIGHT children. Her parents were Abon and Lucille Bridges. She was the oldest of her siblings. The same year that Ruby was born, there was a famous **Supreme Court** case called Brown vs. Board of Education that decided that it was not okay for schools to be segregated. It took over five more years, but eventually the government in certain places started to let Black children go to white schools, and Ruby was one of them. She had to pass a test to get in, and she did. This was huge for Ruby's family and the country, because the government had never done anything like this before. Since the schools had been segregated, this was a great accomplishment. When Ruby grew up, she had four boys, and because of her work she left them a better world to live in.

Ruby Bridges was a Civil Rights activist, which means that she was against people being treated differently just because of their skin color. She showed her activism by being the first Black person to go to the William Frantz Elementary School. This was a big deal because this was also the first school to be integrated in the southern part of the United States. She was in first grade when she first went to William Frantz Elementary School. Her teacher, Barbra Henry, was a really good teacher. She was a very nice teacher, and she supported Ruby. Barbra was amazed at young Ruby's bravery and how Ruby didn't seem to mind what was going on around her. Some white people did not like how well Ruby took how she was being treated. They did not want a Black person to be in a white school, and Ruby knew that. She simply knew that she couldn't let what someone else thought stop her from doing the right thing. The police had to go to school every day with Ruby to make sure that she would not be in danger. The crowd still wanted to do terrible things to Ruby, even though her guards would not let her get hurt. The crowd kept on throwing things at Ruby, and calling her names, but Ruby was **persistent**. In 2014, a statue of Ruby Bridges was placed in the William Frantz Elementary School in her honor.

One of Ruby's greatest accomplishments was creating the Ruby Bridges Foundation, in which Ruby gives lectures and speaks at schools across the country. The Ruby Bridges Foundation also encourages respect for all skin colors, and promotes **anti-racism**. In particular, they also work with the William Frantz School in New Orleans, which she **integrated** in 1960. The project involves making the school a historical site, changing the library, changing the name to Ruby Bridges, and creating a Ruby Bridges Program at the school. She is still alive today creating a bigger difference, and continues to change the world.

The results of Ruby Bridges' work are amazing! She has shaped a new future by helping to **desegregate** schools and make a different, better world. Ruby has set a great example for the rest of us that can be seen in this quote: *"Racism is a grown-up disease and we must stop using our children to spread it."* Which to us means that grown ups should not take advantage of children and pass on their negative views. By reading this you should agree, and we want everybody to follow the footsteps of the amazing, brave, talented Ruby Bridges, who fought for equal rights for all!

Glossary

Access - To be able to have something safely and easily.

Anti-Racism - standing up and speaking out against racism; actively working for racial **equity**.

Civil Rights - People have the right to get the same things, even if they have different skin colors.

Courageous - Someone with lots of bravery.

Black Lives Matter - A social movement as well as a statement standing up for the rights and safety of Black people.

Carbon Footprint - The amount of **pollution** caused by a specific person, group, location or event. This is usually related to how much **fossil fuels** it takes to do something.

Climate Change - The long term effects of temperatures rising and other changes to our planet. This is also sometimes called **global warming**.

Environment - The natural world, either as our whole planet or a particular area. This usually has to do with the health of an environment especially related to how humans impact that. A **habitat** is a specific environment for a certain type of species.

Equality - When two things are equal or two people (or groups) are given the same rights, access, pay or opportunities.

Equity- When everyone has what they need to be happy and successful.

Integration - When a place or group has people from different races or other types of groups. When something is integrated, it is **desegregated**.

Inspire - To help someone else believe in themself or their ability to do something.

Nobel Peace Prize - An award given each year to someone in the world who has done amazing work to create peace and equity.

NGO (Non-Governmental Organization) - A group that is run separately from the government and helps with social or environmental issues.

Perseverance / Persistence - Not giving up, even if what you are doing has some challenges.

Politician - A person who works in government; often politicians are elected to their positions.

Poverty- Not having enough money or resources to meet your basic needs. A person or group in poverty might also be called **disadvantaged.**

Racism - People who are racist don't want people with certain skin colors to have the same rights as others.

Segregation - Places being separated because of people having different skin colors.

Suppression - Stopping or getting in the way of someone having something.

Supreme Court - The most powerful court in the United States of America.

This book was made possible by generous grant funding from the
Ithaca Public Education Initiative

Ithaca Public Education Initiative